contents

Written by Steve Hocking, Anne Dixon and Bridget Caldwell

£5.99 UK only

Left: Katy and Stuart drove a 1901 Mors car in the centenary veteran car run from London to Brighton.

Below: Stuart was bathed in wax as the studio became a health spa. Katy was covered in seaweed – all to keep the body beautiful.

Bottom: Konnie met Simon for his first filming trip – a New Year's Day dip in the Serpentine in London's Hyde Park. This photo was taken before he tried the icy water!

Below: Dr Who's battered old time-travelling machine, the Tardis, made an unexpected landing in the studio.

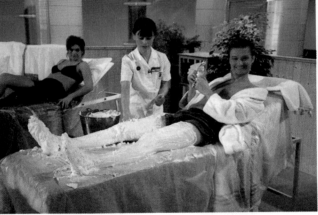

Hello there!

Welcome to the twenty-ninth Blue Peter book. 1999 has been an exciting year for Blue Peter. We're celebrating our forty-first anniversary and have welcomed several new members to our team – including Lucy, our 19th Blue Peter pet. In this book you can find out more about her and all the presenters.

Blue Peter is the longest continuously running children's programme in the world – and we think it's the best! In this book you can find out what makes it so special. Discover how Blue Peter gets on the air, what it takes to be a Blue Peter presenter, and how you can win one of the most prized of all possessions – a Blue Peter badge!

We hope that we have picked some of your favourite Blue Peter moments. We've had great fun choosing them and hope that you will enjoy hours of cooking, making things and reading. We hope you will enter the great competition on page 62. If you win, we look forward to meeting you at the Blue Peter studio!

2000 is a special year, the start of a new millennium. We hope that you will celebrate it with us and will make a date with Blue Peter in the new century, every Monday, Wednesday and Friday.

Above: Simon was taught to walk the tightrope by former presenter Peter Duncan (star of the musical 'Barnum').

Left: Katy met soccer ace Andy Cole as she toured the country with her magic ball.

Katy Hill

Konnie Huq
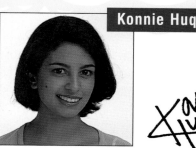

Simon Thomas

Matt Baker

George

Kari

Oke

Mabel

Lucy
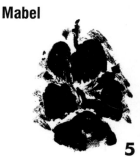

5

MEXICO

'Hola!' That's 'hello' in Spanish, and that's what we said when we arrived in Mexico City. It's the biggest city in the world with a population of 25 million, and, as it's 2,200 metres above sea level, the oxygen is thin and the pollution is dreadful.

The city was built on the bed of a huge lake and is now sinking six centimetres a year – very bad news for the city's historic buildings and landmarks, like the famous Angel of Independence, which is being pushed up out of the ground.

The roads were teeming with bright green classic VW Beetles – they're all taxis and are now only made in Mexico. We jumped into several to explore the city centre before trying another eye-catching form of transport – the brightly coloured Xochmilco boats. We were serenaded along with other locals by a floating Mariachi band as we enjoyed a leisurely punt along the city's ancient Aztec Xochmilco waterway. Later, we had a date at 6 o'clock sharp in the Plaza Garibaldi, where we watched the Mexican flag being lowered, a daily event signifying the end of the day's business and the start of the city's exciting night life.

Mexico is a huge and varied country. One of its most awe-inspiring natural wonders is the Barranca del Cobre or Copper Canyon. It's bigger and deeper than America's Grand Canyon. It's not an easy part of the country to get to, so Stuart

and Konnie drove as far as they could before boarding a train known as 'the donkey' – the only way to go all the way through the canyon. It's a busy daily service that travels slowly along the 300-mile-long Chihuahua-Pacifico railroad, crossing 39 bridges and passing through 86 tunnels, one of which is almost 3 miles long – a real feat of engineering brilliance. The journey only cost £10, but took a very long 12 hours. Stuart had the privilege of standing right on the front of the train, and when it passed through one of the tunnels he felt as though he was burrowing to the centre of the earth!

One of Stuart's most memorable moments was filming on a breathtaking balancing rock which stuck right out over the canyon with a sheer drop on three sides. Legend has it that if you stand on it and make it wobble, all your dreams will come true. And yes, he did it!

Scattered around the vast Copper Canyon live 50,000 Tarahumara Indians – some in caves and others in huts made of clay and wood. Konnie hauled herself on

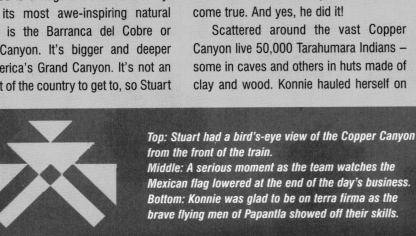

Top: Stuart had a bird's-eye view of the Copper Canyon from the front of the train.
Middle: A serious moment as the team watches the Mexican flag lowered at the end of the day's business.
Bottom: Konnie was glad to be on terra firma as the brave flying men of Papantla showed off their skills.

down Mexico way

Left, from the top:
Konnie eventually
made friends with her
donkey who took her
safely to the
Tarahumara village.

Katy explored the
architectural wonder
of Mexico City's
modern basilica.

Tarahumara children
told Konnie about
their long walk to
school – not returning
to their village in the
Copper Canyon until
the weekend.

Katy and Stuart
posing with a stylish
new VW Beetle.

A rare, relaxed
moment for Katy.

Taxi! There were
thousands of green
beetles roaring along
the streets of
Mexico City.

'Braveheart' Miles pits his thigh against the
locals for an unusual ball game – Ulama.

MEXICO

Below: Sampling a local delicacy – deep-fried crickets!

Above: Stuart explored the deserted mining town of Real de Catorce – rumoured to be haunted!

Far left: La Quebrada divers thrilling the tourists with a death-defying leap.

Left: Wish you were here! Konnie lounging on Acapulco beach.

Below: A lazy afternoon on a Xochimilco boat.

8

Below: Konnie at the ancient
site of Teotihuacan.

*Below: Konnie at the ancient
site of Teotihuacan.*

*Below: Banana leaves make great
brollies in a tropical downpour.*

Above: Baywatch here we come!

*Below: Katy and the Blue Peter
crew take a refreshing dip after
a long, hot day's filming.*

to a mule to cross some bumpy terrain before meeting up with local children, who travel a long way at the beginning and end of each week to attend school outside the canyon.

Tarahumara means 'foot runners' and the Indians are renowned for their long-distance running. One of their most celebrated rituals is a wooden ball game called Ulama. It became popular thousands of years ago and is only played by men. Konnie heaved a sigh of relief, but put her heart and soul into cheering along 'Braveheart' Miles, who joined a team for a game that can sometimes last for weeks! The idea is to hit the wooden ball with your hip – quite a tricky and painful little manoeuvre. Stuart soon got the hang of it and gained the respect of the crowd of cheering fans. That's not all he gained – his hips were black and blue with bruises.

If you think Stuart was brave, Katy was even more impressed with Acapulco's biggest tourist attraction – the world-famous La Quebrada cliff divers. These high divers have become so popular with tourists that, four times a day, they climb to the top of the rocks and wait for a perfect wave before, with split-second timing, diving head first into the

sea over 40 metres below. Katy was amazed that anyone could be so brave and asked one of the divers why he did it. He told her he loved diving but that he always said a prayer at a shrine set into the cliff face which he always passed on his way to the top. In true Blue Peter style, was Katy going to have a go? Not on your life!

The Mexican people are especially proud of their long history and ancient traditions. Konnie found powerful reminders of the Aztecs and the Mayans, the two great civilisations which ruled Mexico long before Europeans arrived almost 500 years ago. In 1519, Mexico was conquered by the Spanish and many people died from diseases brought to Mexico by Hernan Cortés and his soldiers to which the Aztecs had no resistance. The new Spanish rulers banned all old customs and traditions and introduced not only their language but their faith – Catholicism – to the Mexican people.

Fortunately, many of the glories of the Aztecs and the Mayans did survive, and we were grateful to have the chance to see them as well as so much of a fascinating modern Mexico.

PRESENTING → SIMON

BEGINNINGS...

Schools	Grimston Junior and Middle School, Norfolk Aberdour school for Boys and St John's School in Leatherhead, Surrey
Favourite subject	History and Art
Hated subjects	Maths and Chemistry
Qualifications	10 GCSEs, 3 'A' levels, B.A. (Hons) in History from Birmingham University
Earliest ambition	To play professionally for Norwich City Football Club
First acting experience	A Lord in Shakespeare's Richard II
Hobbies when younger	Football, art, photography and bad impersonations
Pets when younger	Cats – Socksy and Moppet Rabbit – Dusty
First job	McDonalds (I only lasted five weeks)

Born	26 January
Height	1.85m
Star sign	Aquarius

THOMAS

FAVOURITES...

Colour	Blue
Best food	My mum's roast lamb
Worst food	Shepherd's pie and Brussels sprouts
Sports	Football, rugby and surfing
Band	The Verve, Embrace, The Corrs
Album	Urban Hymns by the Verve
TV Shows	Eastenders, A Question of Sport, Cold Feet, Alan Partridge
Star	Robin Williams
Best Movie	Dead Poets' Society and Saving Private Ryan
Clothes	Summer clothes – jeans and short-sleeved shirts
Best ways to spend Saturdays	Staying in bed watching Live and Kicking then going to see Norwich City play

"My feet haven't hit the ground since I joined the programme!" says Simon. "I used to watch Blue Peter when I was younger and would sit there thinking 'I'd love to do that one day'. One of my favourite presenters was Peter Duncan, so it was great to team up with him in the musical, 'Barnum'. As it's a show all about the circus, Peter taught me how to walk the tightrope. He even let me come on and juggle at the end of the show. I practised hard all day, walked out in front of the audience and ... dropped the balls!"

Simon hasn't looked back since. But if anyone thinks that being a Blue Peter presenter is a glamorous job, Simon's quick to point out that his first filming experience was jumping into the icy water of the Serpentine in London's Hyde Park for a swimming race. "It was freezing! What people don't realise is that I had to do it twice. After finishing the race, I was inside warming up, when the director came in and told me I had to do it again – the crew had just realised there was a problem with the camera. At first I thought he was joking, but I quickly realised he wasn't!"

A Blue Peter presenter's life is a busy one. "You never know what you're going to be doing next. So far, I've raced huskies, learnt how to scuba-dive, abseiled down a cliff to put up a birdwatching camera, learnt how to flamenco dance and trained with the England under-18 football team. Not a bad job!"

TOMORROW...

Most wants to do on BP	Fly with the Red Arrows, go white-water rafting and sky-diving
Country most wants to visit	India
People most respect	My parents and charity workers
Bad habit	Very bad at keeping rooms tidy
Ambition	To live every day as if it might be my last

SIMON'S

First things first – collect the key...

Friday 8 January 1999 will be a day that Simon will never forget – it was his first appearance on Blue Peter. And the BP cameras were there to capture his every move!

...this must be mine.

Simon's first day on Blue Peter started at 9 o'clock sharp when he walked into the BBC's Television Centre to collect his dressing room key from the Stage Door. Feeling rather nervous, he made his way to Studio 4 where the crew was already busy getting ready for the show.

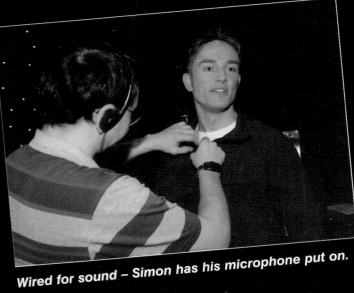
Wired for sound – Simon has his microphone put on.

Konnie shows Simon his Blue Peter badge.

FIRST DAY

Time to check the script with Helen on portaprompt.

The gang watch Simon's audition film.

Ten o'clock and time to start rehearsing. The floor manager showed Simon his positions and which cameras would be taking his close-ups! Stuart, Katy and Konnie passed on lots of helpful tips – they could all remember their first day.

During Simon's audition, he said sky-diving was something he really wanted to try. His wish was going to come true – well almost! The production team had booked a free-fall simulator for the Friday Challenge! The simulator was so big it had to be set up outside the studio. Simon had plenty of time to get the hang of it and was beginning to enjoy himself.

It's up, up and away as Simon gets in a bit of practice on the simulator.

13

Decision time – what shall I wear?

Karen, Blue Peter's make-up designer, makes up Simon.

After lunch, pop band Another Level arrived in the studio and started rehearsing their song. This gave Simon a chance to visit make-up and wardrobe to sort out what to wear for the show.

Two minutes until live transmission. It was nearly ten past five and there was no turning back. Trying to feel confident, Simon got ready for the start of the show and the team wished him luck. Then the 'on air' sign lit up. Seconds later, disaster struck. The simulator wasn't working because of torrential rain. Nothing was going to be the way Simon and the rest of the team expected. But as they say, the show must go on.

Would the new Blue Peter presenter please reveal himself?

The first half wasn't too bad – all Simon had to do was stand behind a screen being the mystery new presenter. A film featuring Simon and three other hopefuls' auditions was shown and then the moment arrived. "So who's it going to be? Will the new Blue Peter presenter please reveal himself?". Right on cue, Simon smashed through the paper screen and presented himself to Blue Peter's five million viewers.

Time to meet an important member of the team – Mabel!

After meeting the four-legged members of the team – Bonnie, Mabel, Kari and Oke – Katy pinned on Simon's badge. He'd done it – Simon Thomas was officially the 27th Blue Peter presenter.

Bye-bye BONNIE

Born on 3 February 1986, Bonnie had showbiz in her blood. Blue Peter's Goldie was her mum and Bonnie was one of eight pups from her second litter.

Bonnie's father was a Guide Dogs for the Blind stud dog so everyone had high hopes for the pups. They all qualified as trainee Guide Dogs but Bonnie was extra-special and we kept her for the programme.

66,368 viewers sent in suggestions for the puppies' names and the most popular were chosen. Apart from Bonnie, there was Halley, Bonzo, Honey, Fergie, Snowy, Amber and Bruno.

Bonnie made her first appearance in the studio when she was six weeks old and became top dog when her mother retired in the summer of 1986 and Simon Groom left the show.

In January 1991 Bonnie became a mum herself. Six lively bundles of blonde fur were soon frolicking in front of the TV cameras. We kept in touch with the litter and organised a grand birthday reunion when Bonnie was ten.

Anthea Turner and Bonnie got on famously and the highlight of both their Blue Peter careers was being Showbiz Agility Champion two years running!

Cards sent by (from left to right) Lucy and Ben Archer, Blyton Wilson, Katy Thomas, Laura Sloan and David Willis.

In 1996 when RSPCA rescue dog Mabel joined the team, Bonnie didn't bat an eyelid even though Mabel was a minx! It's thanks to Bonnie's calming and stable influence that Mabel has become such a good dog.

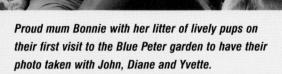

Proud mum Bonnie with her litter of lively pups on their first visit to the Blue Peter garden to have their photo taken with John, Diane and Yvette.

After taking part in 1,150 programmes with 16 different presenters, Bonnie deserved a well-earned rest. At 13, equivalent to 91 in human years, Bonnie was in very good health but was not enjoying walking on our slippery studio floor. She much prefers snuggling up on a rug or lying out in the sunshine at Leonie Pocock's home in Surrey. Leonie has looked after Bonnie since she was a tiny puppy so she's bound to have a very enjoyable and peaceful retirement.

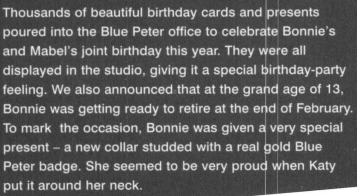

Above: Bonnie was a great mum and her pups soon put on weight and started scampering around.
Right: Vet Jo Inglis has been a long-standing fan.

Thousands of beautiful birthday cards and presents poured into the Blue Peter office to celebrate Bonnie's and Mabel's joint birthday this year. They were all displayed in the studio, giving it a special birthday-party feeling. We also announced that at the grand age of 13, Bonnie was getting ready to retire at the end of February. To mark the occasion, Bonnie was given a very special present – a new collar studded with a real gold Blue Peter badge. She seemed to be very proud when Katy put it around her neck.

Are You Being Served?

MATERIALS

You will need: large grocery box, card or paint for the walls and floor, shoebox for the changing cubicle, food-bag box, cereal packet, cardboard tube, glue, silver sticky tape, silver paint, silver card or foil, a mirror, three straws, coloured paper, curtain material, curtain rings, empty matchbox, paper clips, pump-action bottle tops, garden wire, plastic tub for hangers, screw cap, computer pictures, an old doll and modelling clay.

FOR THE SHOP cut away one long side of a strong grocery box. Trim the cut-away side so that it will cover the base of the box, making an extra-firm floor. If necessary, cut the three remaining sides down to the height that suits your dolls.

You can then paint or cover the walls with coloured card. Do the same for the floor unless you can find a piece of leftover carpet or material to glue in place.

THE CHANGING CUBICLE is made from a shoebox. Cut off one of the ends and put it aside for the floor. Then cover the box inside and out to match the walls of the shop. Don't bother to cover the underside of the cubicle as this will be hidden. Cover the cut-away end of the box with material and glue it to the floor.

THE CURTAIN POLE is made from a length of drinking-straw covered with silver sticky tape. If you haven't got tape, a long strip of foil works just as well as long as you glue it in place at each end of the straw. The discs that hold the pole in place are made from three or four layers of cardboard. Glue the layers together, cover with foil and make a hole in the middle.

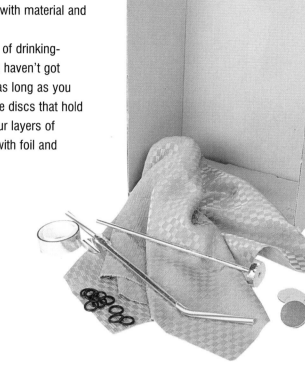

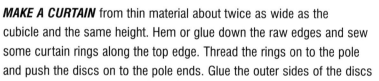

MAKE A CURTAIN from thin material about twice as wide as the cubicle and the same height. Hem or glue down the raw edges and sew some curtain rings along the top edge. Thread the rings on to the pole and push the discs on to the pole ends. Glue the outer sides of the discs to the inside corners of the cubicle. You can glue the cubicle in place or leave it free-standing in case you want to change things around.

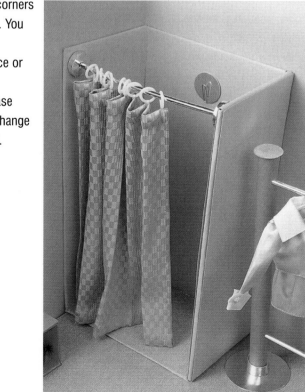

FOR THE ROUND CLOTHES STAND paint or cover a length of cardboard tube. To make the base, cut out a large disc of silver card, or foil-covered card. Draw a circle in the centre the same diameter as the tube and cut slits from the centre to the edge of the drawn circle. Then bend these tabs outwards. Spread glue round one end of the tube and push the disc down to it, pressing the cut sections on to the glue. Check that the tube stands up straight. To cover the jagged edges, glue a strip of card around them. Then glue another strip of card around the tube fairly near the top which will make a ridge for the hanging shelf to sit on. The shelf is a disc of card a little smaller than the base, again with a hole cut out of the middle. Push paper fasteners on to the edge of the disc, leaving them sticking out a little so that the clothes hangers will fit into them. Then push the disc on to the tube until it meets the card strip. To neaten the top, glue a circle of card over the open end of the tube.

THE COUNTER can be made from the lower part of a cereal packet. Use a ruler and mark the height you want for your doll before cutting it. The bottom of the packet becomes the counter top. Decorate the counter by covering it in plain or patterned paper. The top is strengthened by covering it with coloured card.

FOR THE TALL CLOTHES RAIL, make the two upright poles from oblongs of paper about 25 x 20 cm in size. Spread glue down one long side then roll it, fairly tightly, from the unglued edge to the glued one. Press the glued edge down firmly. The actual hanging rails are made from drinking-straws that fit into holes in the poles – one near the top and the other nearer the bottom. The holes should be in line with each other otherwise the stand will be crooked. Cut out two discs of silver card or foil-covered card for the base.

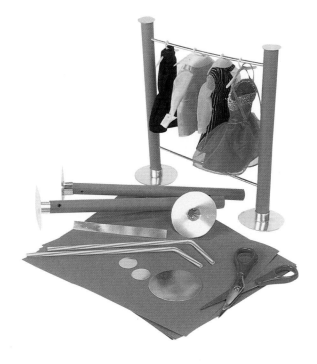

Draw circles in the centre of each disc using the pole as a pattern. From the middle cut out to the line you have drawn and bend back the tabs. Put the poles in the middle of the discs, again gluing the tabs down. Wrap a strip of card around the poles to cover the jagged edges. Wrap foil or sticky tape around the drinking-straws to make them look like chrome hanging rails.

THE MIRROR AND STORAGE BASE. The base is made from a small food-bag box. Cut off the lid and cover the box inside and out with coloured paper.

A tiny mirror with a silver frame resting on the base will give your doll a full-length view of herself. You may want to stick the mirror on the wall with a little Blu-tack.

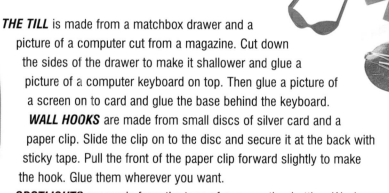

THE TILL is made from a matchbox drawer and a picture of a computer cut from a magazine. Cut down the sides of the drawer to make it shallower and glue a picture of a computer keyboard on top. Then glue a picture of a screen on to card and glue the base behind the keyboard.

WALL HOOKS are made from small discs of silver card and a paper clip. Slide the clip on to the disc and secure it at the back with sticky tape. Pull the front of the paper clip forward slightly to make the hook. Glue them wherever you want.

SPOTLIGHTS are made from the tops of pump-action bottles. Wash and paint them and push a length of foil-covered garden wire into the thin end. Bend the other end of the wire to hang them on the wall.

MAKE CARRIER BAGS from gift paper and tape. Screw caps painted silver make useful **TRAYS** for holding hair accessories. **HANGERS** are cut out from an empty margarine or ice-cream container.

Finally, for a **MODEL FIGURE**, if you have a really old doll that you don't play with any more, take off the head and use the body to show off some of the clothes on sale. Push the feet into a lump of modelling clay so that it will stand up. Then push the clay on to a piece of cardboard and cover it with a circle of card.

KONNIE – Going Home

"This year I was given many challenges. I was asked to ice-skate and 'fin swim' and to 'paramotor fly', but my biggest challenge was a personal one. In April, I was given the chance to make a journey that my parents made 35 years ago – only this time in reverse. This was a chance to learn more about a country I hadn't visited since I was 14."

Konnie flew to Bangladesh – not in luxury – but as part of a team of flight attendants on a scheduled flight. Weeks of training were crammed into 2 days as Konnie learned what it takes to fly 400 passengers on a Boeing 747 in comfort and safety.

Former Blue Peter presenter Janet Ellis had made the same journey 16 years previously. She had visited the Sreepur Children's Village, a home for many of the poorest children in Bangladesh. Konnie returned to the home and discovered that it had changed completely. The home had been demolished and rebuilt, but it still cared for hundreds of children!

"The Sreepur Children's Village has been a fantastic success," says Konnie. **"It's brought hope and the chance of a better life to thousands of children."**

Konnie travelled around Dhaka, the capital city of Bangladesh, with her uncle Rocku.

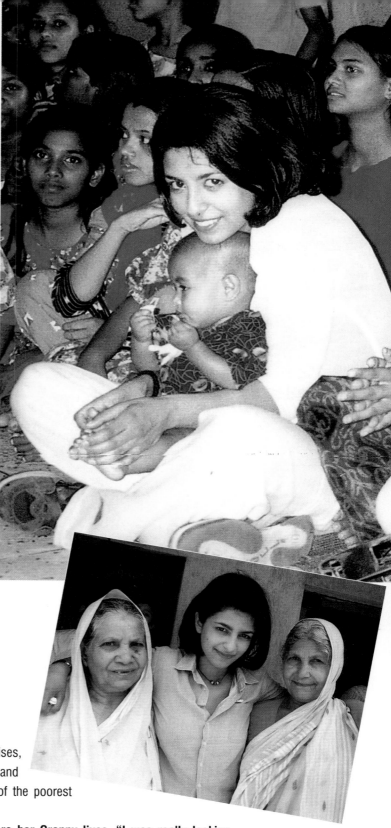

Opposite page, bottom left: Konnie with Pat Kerr and some of the children of the Sreepur village.
Top left: There was a huge family reunion at Konnie's granny's home and everyone enjoyed a celebratory meal.
Below: Konnie with her dad who was also visiting his relatives.

Rocku had also met Janet when he worked for the charity Oxfam!

"Dhaka is always colourful and busy and full of different noises, smells, sights and sounds," says Konnie. She visited a huge fruit and vegetable market, explored the old back streets and met some of the poorest people in the city, living by the main railway.

From Dhaka, Konnie travelled to the village of Pabna, where her Granny lives. "I was really looking forward to seeing my Granny again and I wanted to see her village. I wanted to know how things had changed since my last visit!"

Above: A big cuddle from Konnie for her two grannies.

Konnie met dozens of members of her family, many of whom she hadn't seen for years. "A homecoming is an important event in Bangladesh. Relations that I had never met before had gone to a great deal of trouble to make me feel welcome. It's one thing to meet long-lost relations, and another to meet fifty of them at once, to prepare a feast with them, to be their guest of honour, and have all this filmed at the same time!"

"It was an amazing visit," says Konnie. "Britain is my home, but having strong links with family and friends in Bangladesh is very important to me. When I have children of my own I want to make sure that they also know all about Bangladesh."

1998 BLUE PETER APPEAL

Katy travelled to the remote Gurue district in the north of Mozambique where children often walk for miles each way to get the most basic education. Sonia and Lucinda, here with Katy, are the lucky ones and are pupils in one of the few schools in the area. Lucinda is desperate to become a teacher. Without our Blue Peter Appeal there wouldn't be any more schools built for a very long time. What Mozambique desperately needs are more schools, and thanks to the Blue Peter New Future Appeal and all your hard work, that's exactly what will happen.

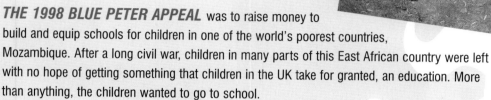

THE 1998 BLUE PETER APPEAL was to raise money to build and equip schools for children in one of the world's poorest countries, Mozambique. After a long civil war, children in many parts of this East African country were left with no hope of getting something that children in the UK take for granted, an education. More than anything, the children wanted to go to school.

We worked with Oxfam, the well-known charity. They wanted to build the schools and we wanted Blue Peter viewers to help them. We aimed to collect enough aluminium foil and cans to pay for and equip three schools – an ambitious target. We wanted to collect 500 tons of aluminium, twice as much as we had ever asked viewers to collect before! All over Britain families collected aluminium. People danced the 'Can Can' in kitchens and playgrounds from Aylesbury to Wokingham as cans were crushed and bagged.

It was the first time we had collected aluminium foil. Separate bags of yoghurt tops and take-away containers piled up at collection points at supermarkets and Oxfam shops around the country. This was one of the biggest foil recycling campaigns ever seen in the UK. Blue Peter viewers recycled 14% of all the foil recycled in the UK in 1998 – a staggering achievement! The foil gave the recycling teams a major headache as warehouses filled up – how could they unbag and process all of it before the appeal ended? As no one had seen this amount of recycled foil before, what would it weigh? Frantic calls from the Blue Peter office to Appeal HQ saw the totaliser rise slowly, but surely.

Huge donations boosted the total, from an aluminium fuel container in Hull to the 'lollipop' sticks from crossing patrols in Nottinghamshire. At the end of February, as collection points closed, Appeal HQ made the call to say that

they were sure that we had collected enough aluminium to fund the schools that were so badly needed. The celebrations began, but nowhere more enthusiastically than in Gurue, where work started in June on the second of the schools.

ALL DRESSED UP ...

Bjorn Again – looking like super troopers from the seventies.

Night watchman Thomas on the roof of St Paul's Cathedral keeping watch over London just as thousands did during World War II.

Holy smoke – it's Batman and Robin.

Bat Hound – even Mabel got dressed in a stylish cape.

BLUE PETER 2108

Imagine Blue Peter in the future... Katy aged 137 with Futura (alias Sarah Greene).

Katy played her great-great-granddaughter in the year 2108.

Mark Curry, Keeper of the memory machine – Konnie went back in time and remembered what she was like aged 14.

King Charles I just before he lost his head.

Back In Time For Christmas. A special pantomime with Blue Peter stars past and present.

Two hundred years ago this hairstyle was all the rage. The style was called the giraffe. Katy wasn't too sure about it but Stuart seemed to approve!

Konnie showing off her stylish safety gear before trying sledge hockey with the Cardiff Huskies.

Simon looked the part dressed as leader of the Roundheads, Oliver Cromwell.

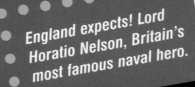

England expects! Lord Horatio Nelson, Britain's most famous naval hero.

PICADILLO

If you want to rustle up a taste of Mexico, you couldn't find a more delicious recipe than Picadillo. It's really easy to make and if you go easy on the chillies, it won't blow your socks off either.

To feed four hungry people you will need:

450g minced beef
oil for frying
1 onion – finely chopped
1 eating apple – peeled, cored and chopped
handful of raisins
small can chopped tomatoes (220g)
1 chilli – seeded and chopped
salt and pepper
good pinch of cinnamon and cumin
1 clove of garlic

• To make Picadillo, start by heating a little oil in a pan and then add the onion and garlic. Toss them around in the oil and add the beef. Stir the ingredients together and keep going until the beef has browned.
• Next add the apple, raisins, tomatoes and 1 jalapeno chilli – 2 if you like hot and spicy food.
Stir everything together and add a little salt and pepper. A good pinch of cinnamon and one of cumin will turn this into a Mexican marvel. Mix well and leave it on a low heat without a lid for around 20-25 minutes. Stir occasionally until the meat is cooked.
• To make an optional extra crunch topping, fry some almond flakes in a small lump of butter. They'll soon turn golden brown.
• Serve the Picadillo with the fried almonds sprinkled on top. To complete this Mexican meal, serve with tortilla chips or rice on the side.
• If you're a vegetarian, this recipe will work well with soya mince or Quorn.

P.S. Wash your hands thoroughly after chopping chillies.

AN INTERVIEW WITH...

STEPS

What do you remember about your first appearance on Blue Peter?

(CLAIRE) "It was our first big live television show so I think we were all a little bit nervous. We'd done a couple of very small TV shows which were live, but never something as important as Blue Peter."

What have you been up to this year?

(LISA) "It seems like we've been all over the world but the main thing we did was to go on tour. It was our first major tour and it was the best experience – we can't wait to get back on the road again."

What's your favourite track on the new album?

(LEE) "There is a track that I really like – it's called 'Deeper Shade of Blue' and it's quite mature but it's still Steps!"

Can we expect some more catchy dance movements?

(FAYE) "Of course! Every Steps single will always have its own little dance – we've just learnt the new dance for the new single and it's the best yet!"

You're about to go on tour again. What are you looking forward to?

(H) "Seeing the audience and meeting the fans. It's what being in a band is all about. Sometimes we have to rush about from place to place and we haven't got time to stop and chat, but I much prefer it when we have a couple of minutes to say a hello to everyone."

Armed with a long list of searching questions, Stuart grills the million album-selling act Steps he gets the chance to write for *Big!* magazine.

What was the recent tour like?

(LISA) "It was the most fantastic experience. The best thing was the reaction of the audiences all over the UK – our fans are the greatest!"

What have been your highlights so far?

(CLAIRE) "The Brits was really excellent! That and the *Smash Hits* Poll Winners Party last year where we performed 'Tragedy'. And having our first No. 1, of course."

Who are your musical heroes?

(LEE) "People like George Michael and Robbie Williams – they are the kind of artists I admire."

What are your ambitions?

(LEE) "My personal ambitions are to sky-dive – I really want to do that – and just to keep on getting more successful."

Does anyone have any annoying habits?

(FAYE) "H is the member of Steps with the habits – he has enough for the rest of us put together. Some of them are too disgusting to mention but we all love him really!"

5, 6, 7, 8 – Steps' first single was performed live in the Blue Peter studio in 1997 – line dancing was suddenly top of the pops.

What's been your favourite dance routine so far?
(LISA) "I really like 'Love's Got a Hold on my Heart" because it flows really well. I've got dance training so I'm maybe more conscious of what works and what doesn't."

What's been the most memorable appearance on Blue Peter?
(H) "The one where we opened the show with 'Heartbeat' and got to do a bit of presenting. That was brilliant!"

What do you do in your spare time?
(LEE) "I go to the gym, read books, that kind of thing. The girls tend to go shopping – Faye and Lisa will go clubbing and Claire will watch a video. H also goes shopping and sees friends."

What do you like watching on television?
(CLAIRE) "We don't get enough time to watch TV, but we all like 'Friends'. And, of course, 'Blue Peter'!"

I know Stuart interviewed you, how d'ya think he did?
(H) "He did very well until the end when he forgot his tape! Seriously, he's a very talented presenter."

How are you planning to celebrate the millennium?
(LISA) "Hopefully we'll be performing at a huge show with all our friends and family in the audience. Otherwise, it'll be a party somewhere!"

Steps became an overnight sensation and luckily for Blue Peter viewers this fivesome are always keen to return to our studio. They even sang specially for Stuart on his last show.

33

Below left: One day old with her mum and brothers and sisters.
Below right: Exploring the great outdoors.

Lovely Lucy!

LUCY'S EARLY LIFE

Our 19th pet came into the world on 14 September 1998. She was a beautiful Golden Retriever whose Mum, Indi, is a fully trained field-trial dog and whose Dad, Lillingdessi, is one of a long line of show dogs, making her a pedigree. There were eight pups in the litter but Lucy was the one chosen by Leonie Pocock, who thought she'd be a perfect pal for Bonnie and Mabel.

Lucy stayed with her Mum until she was almost 8 weeks old, and had her vaccinations at 9 weeks, followed by an all-over vet check at 12 weeks. Naturally, she was given full marks! It's very important to see a puppy with its mother, as this helps to judge its adult appearance and temperament.

Lucy was soon on the rampage in the garden, sniffing the plants and finding toys to play with. Young pups love to chew, so it's good to give them something of their own, like an old knotted tea towel, before they get their teeth into your slippers!

Bonnie kept a watchful eye on Lucy, and after 13 weeks it was time to get out and about to meet other dogs. Lucy wanted to be friends with everything on four legs.

LUCY MAKES HER DEBUT

Lucy made her debut on Blue Peter on **Monday 22 February,** which was also Bonnie's last studio appearance. Little Lucy wasn't quite so little any more, but was an instant hit with everyone at Television Centre and was a natural in front of the cameras. After her first live programme, her fan mail started pouring in – yes, you loved her too!

Simon is already attending dog-training classes with Lucy. It's a team effort, as dogs are only ever as good as their owners. Lucy is keen to learn and we're sure she'll pass her Good Citizenship test with flying colours.

Second from top: "Pleased to meet you, Oke."

Above: Lucy's first Christmas.

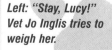

Left: "Stay, Lucy!" Vet Jo Inglis tries to weigh her.

Lucy

Make your very own BLUE PETER DOGS

For keen collectors of bean-filled animals – here come the Blue Peter canines! Not available in the shops, but follow these instructions, and you can create your very own.

MATERIALS

➜ White towelling for Mabel and golden-coloured for Bonnie and Lucy
➜ Split peas
➜ Strong sewing thread
➜ Black wool and black paint (for Mabel)
➜ Scraps of felt or paper for noses, eyes and tongues
➜ Ribbon for collars
➜ Paper for patterns and rubber solution glue

Start by making a pattern for the body. Fold an 18 cm square of paper in half. At one end, starting about 5 cm from the folded edge, draw a slanting line to half-way along the folded long side. Cut away the spare paper outside the drawn line, unfold it, and you have the pattern.

Pin the edges of the pattern on to your towelling and cut it out.

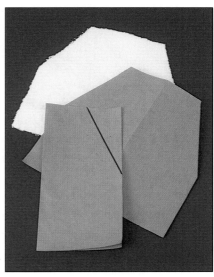

37

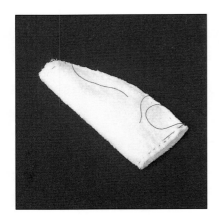

Fold the towelling in half with the shaped sides together. Stitch the shaped sides using fairly small stitches so that the filling won't fall out.

Then, at the top and bottom edges, sew straight stitches all round. Do not sew the two thicknesses together. Pull up the thread tightly at the bottom, wider edge and oversew firmly.

Turn the body right side out and you won't see any ugly stitching. Be warned, this is fiddly, as the neck is narrow.

Fill the body with split peas. If you cut the top from a plastic drinks bottle, it forms a perfect funnel and makes filling easier. Then pull up the stitches around the neck, thread a needle and oversew firmly.

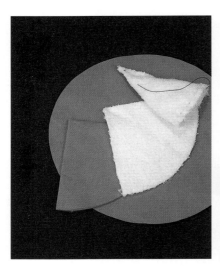

To make the head, draw round a dinner plate to make a paper pattern. Cut it out and fold in half twice. You'll end up with a fan shape. Pin it on to towelling and cut it out. Fold in half and sew the straight sides together. Sew all around the curved edge and leave a long thread.

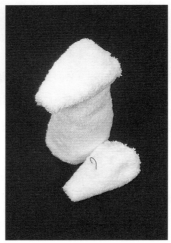

Turn right side out, leaving the tip inside to give a straight end to the muzzle.

Fill the head with split peas and gather up the open end and oversew.

About half-way down the head sew a few stitches through the head from front to back. Pull up the stitches tightly and instantly the face will become the right shape.

Push the neck end of the body down inside itself to hide rough edges and stitches. Spread glue around the folded edge and push the head into place. The seam in the body should be where the spine would be.

The ears are two triangles. Make Bonnie's and Lucy's more rounded. Put a little glue around the cut edges to stop the towelling fraying. Glue one edge of each ear to the head. If you're making Mabel, stick one pointing up and the other folded down.

The nose is a small triangular shape with the corners rounded off. Cut out in felt or paper and glue in place. Eyes are split peas painted black and glued on to circles of paper. Glue in place. Tongues are filled-in U shapes cut from pink felt or paper. Glue the straight end inside the muzzle.

Legs are made from oblongs about 5 x 10 cm in size. Fold one long side over the other and glue down. Gather up one end for the paw with a few stitches and either

glue or sew the paw in place so that it stays at right angles to the leg. Glue the tops of the legs to the front of the body.

The tail is a strip of material narrowing at one end. Glue or sew one edge over the other, making the tip as small as possible. Glue in place under the body. For Mabel's markings cut up some strands of black wool and keep snipping until it becomes fluff. Spread some glue, a little at a time, where the markings are to be and press on the wool fluff. When the glue is dry trim off any loose bits.

Collars are lengths of ribbon with discs made from scraps of foil. To be realistic, you could cut out a small gold shape and attach to Bonnie's collar to look like her gold Blue Peter badge.

1999 saw the 175th birthday of an organisation that Blue Peter has supported for many years. The Royal National Lifeboat Institution, or RNLI, raises all its income from members of the public, including generations of Blue Peter viewers.

→ THE RNLI
175 YEARS OF SAVING LIVES

The RNLI was founded in 1824 to give help to sailors in danger around the coast of Britain and Ireland. Since then it has saved 132,785 lives. There are 223 lifeboat stations. Boats at seven stations have been bought as result of four Blue Peter Appeals. The first Blue Peter lifeboats were launched in 1967. They have put to sea over three thousand times.

Blue Peter 1 is stationed at Littlehampton, Blue Peter 2 at Beaumaris, Blue Peter 3 at North Berwick, and Blue Peter 4 at St Agnes, in Cornwall. These were the four original Blue Peter lifeboat stations. Since then three more have been added, at Portaferry in County Down, at Cleethorpes, and at Fishguard in Pembrokeshire. Simon spent a day in Fishguard with the crew of Blue Peter 7.

The day started with Simon running with the other crew members to the lifeboat. Apart from the full-time coxswain and mechanic, the crew

"Simon Thomas reporting for duty." Simon takes the controls of Blue Peter VII.

Left: Hundreds of thousands of paperback books, buttons, postcards and unwanted metal objects have kept Blue Peter lifeboats in action for over 30 years. Right: We've featured all our lifeboats and met their crews in 32 years of work with the RNLI.

members are all volunteers – they have jobs in the town but must be ready to stop everything they are doing and race to the station as soon as they are called, whatever the time of day or night, and whatever the weather. They aim to have the boat at sea within 10 minutes. Simon found out just how fast you have to be to respond to the call, and to put on the special waterproof suits that all lifeboat men and women wear.

"I didn't want to be the last one to the boat," says Simon, "but I was!" Once Simon and the crew were aboard the lifeboat, Deputy Second Coxswain Paul Butler put to sea. Paul let Simon take the controls. "Speed saves lives," says Simon. "The crew don't waste a second getting people out of the water once they've found them. I had no idea lifeboats could travel so fast!"

Simon took part in a training exercise. He was dropped over the side of the lifeboat to help an RAF rescue helicopter practise the sort of manoeuvre needed to rescue a 'man overboard'. "It was very cold in the water," says Simon. "No one could last long in those conditions, and we were filming on a nice, calm day! The water was absolutely freezing. It was great to see the lifeboat returning to pick me up. You can see why the lifeboat crews have to do so much training."

The Blue Peter lifeboats have saved over 900 lives since they were first launched – that means there are 900 people alive today who might have died without the support of Blue Peter viewers.

175 years of saving lives at sea

It was a rough ride!

Can you spot the tiny camera on the front of my bike? It filmed me in close-up over all the bumps!

KATY HILL

One of the great things about presenting Blue Peter is that you get the chance to have a go at almost everything! Katy had never ridden a motorbike, and that seemed a challenge too good to miss.

Katy travelled to Chippenham in Wiltshire to meet leading rider Dave Thorpe. Dave has been the world motocross champion three times. He coaches many of Britain's youngest and best riders. Who better to teach Katy the basics?

Over 4,000 young people take part in motocross each weekend. Riders race around specially built off-road circuits. They must be fast, and very skilful. The courses are full of corners, can be very muddy and have spectacular jumps.

Early in the morning Katy was fitted out with all the equipment needed to ride a motocross bike safely – helmet, protective padding, gloves and strong boots. She was ready to go! The secret to riding a motorbike is getting the engine running at the right speed to change from one gear to another. When you've mastered the clutch you can get moving, slowly at first, then moving up the gears. After a few false starts, Katy was off.

Motocross circuits are bumpy, so you get a painful ride if you sit down. However, as Katy discovered, riding the bike isn't that easy when you're standing up, either!

There are different classes of bikes, according to the size of the engine. Katy was a new rider and so hers was an 80cc bike, but the serious competitors had much more powerful ones. Top bikers reach speeds of up to seventy miles per hour and they can jump up to seven metres into the air.

ACTION GIRL!

By the afternoon Dave thought Katy had learned enough to have a go at riding with other motorcyclists. Some of the top young riders in Britain gave Katy a head start. *"I have to admit it was scary with so many bikes whizzing past me,"* says Katy. *"I thought I did quite well, but of course, the others were soon way ahead!"*

A few falls soon showed why the protective padding is so necessary, as Katy says: *"Driving any kind of motorbike is dangerous. It's very important to get proper training and wear all the protective clothing. As I found out!"* No harm done, but along with great memories, Katy brought some spectacular bruises back to the office!

Protective clothing is essential for this sport – and there was plenty of it.

43

Dear Blue Peter...

I made the clothes shop that you made on your show. I made it with the help of my two friends Ellen and Joanna, and we also made a shoe cupboard to store things in. I have enjoyed playing with it and I always enjoy the show. May I have your autographs please?

Sarah (aged 9)

We thought you'd like to see this photograph of the Snowmen Christmas Table Decoration which we made after seeing it on the show. To finish it off, our mum helped us cut out a section of the wadding and stick a piece of silver paper below it to make a lake. We have kept it carefully for next year. We love your show and never miss it. Our mum and dad watched Blue Peter (John Noakes and Valerie Singleton) when they were wee.

Emma (aged 9) and Mark (aged 8)

We thought you might like to see our collection of Blue Peter books. We have got most of them from charity shops for £1 or less. Our oldest books are from 1965 and 1966. Numbers 6, 7 and 10 were our mum's when she was a girl.

Lawrence (aged 9),
Gregory (aged 8)
and Robert (aged 5)

We made Blue Peter dogs out of the instructions that Konnie used. It took you about ten minutes on the programme but it took us about four hours! But we still enjoyed it because it was a really great idea.

John (aged 8 1/2), Claire (aged 9) and Lorna (aged 4 1/2)

After watching the programme at Easter where you made the Easter card using a flannel, I decided to make one for grandma and grandpa with a yellow rabbit and some green tufts of grass that I made from two different flannels.

Charlotte (aged 10)

We made Advent Calendars in all different shapes – a Christmas bauble, a stocking and a tree. We enjoyed making them.

Ian (aged 8), Jenny (aged 6) and Mark (aged 3)

Here is my Blue Peter Advent Calendar. I hope you like it!

Katy (aged 7)

My sister and I made this Christmas ring while watching Blue Peter at our nana's house and I thought you would like to see it. It is still hanging in nana's kitchen and she keeps eating the sweets!

Gemma (aged 9) and Megan (aged 6)

This is a picture of me and the barometer model that we have made – it works really well!

Sophie (aged 6) and Sean (aged 5)

I liked your idea for the jewellery so I made up some badges for members to wear at my club house. I hope you like this idea.

Thomas (aged 8)

I thought you might like to see a photograph of my 'split-pea' dog which I made. I watched your programme when you made a dog like Mabel from towelling and split peas. I decided to make a dog like my cocker spaniel Benjie, who is also in the photo. I have called my dog 'Konnie' as I was lucky enough to meet Konnie and get her autograph at the Big Bash.

Jennie (aged 9)

It was a celebration to beat all others. BBC2 devoted an entire evening to the programme, with Blue Peter Night. But on Blue Peter's 40th birthday, 16 October 1998, we invited presenters from all four decades to help get us in the party mood.

From the nineties there were Diane Louise Jordan, Anthea Turner, Tim Vincent and John Leslie.

Representing the eighties were Yvette Fielding, Caron Keating, Mark Curry, Janet Ellis, Peter Duncan, Sarah Greene, Tina Heath, Simon Groom and Christopher Wenner.

Presenters from the sixties and seventies were Valerie Singleton, John Noakes and Peter Purves. There was a big welcome to Leila Williams who presented the very first Blue Peter programme.

We organised everyone into teams for party games. The Glue Pot Gladiators were captained by Katy, The Advent Crown Adventurers were led by Richard, and the Sticky Tape Superstars had Konnie in charge. The star prize was a golden squeezy bottle.

Competition was fierce and frantic as each team tried their hand at motorised barrel racing, pancake tossing, plate spinning and finally the biggest challenge of all – getting ready for a party in double quick time. There was dressing up followed by bouncing balloons, wrapping presents, icing a cake and, lastly, glitter decorating a card. The winners? Queen of the glue pot, Katy, and her Gladiators team of John Noakes, Tina, Janet, Sarah, Caron and John Leslie.

Our twenty-five-minute party whizzed by and it was an emotional goodbye from everyone as we sliced up a whopping birthday cake and everyone wondered whether they might be asked back for Blue Peter's fiftieth!

How many presenters can you identify in the group picture opposite? Answers on page 63.

> *"The star prize was a golden squeezy bottle!"*

BLUE PETER'S

40TH BIRTHDAY!

Simon's Family Album

If you really want to get to know someone, you need the inside info. There's no better place to start than with a family photo album. Simon bravely let us take a peek inside and here are just a few of his family's treasured snaps that tell the whole truth and nothing but the truth...

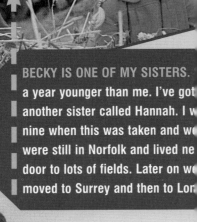

BECKY IS ONE OF MY SISTERS. a year younger than me. I've got another sister called Hannah. I w nine when this was taken and we were still in Norfolk and lived ne door to lots of fields. Later on we moved to Surrey and then to Lon

FISHING WAS A BIG HOBBY of mine – I never used to catch very much, although my friend and I did once catch a pike. It had such sharp teeth that neither of us wanted to pull the hook out! I always put the fish back in the water afterwards though.

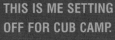

THIS IS ME SETTING OFF FOR CUB CAMP. I was eight years old and living in Norfolk. We moved around a lot because my dad was a vicar. There was a lot of open country-side nearby and camp wasn't far away. I didn't last long in the Scouts though, as I preferred playing five-a-side football.

HERE I AM ON HOLIDAY IN CROMER with my little sister. We lived there until I was three. Later we used to go back there for holidays in the cottage we had there.

4

5

SETTING OUT FOR MY FIRST DAY AT SENIOR SCHOOL in a very new uniform. My favourite subjects were English, history and art. I couldn't stand science or maths classes.

I USED TO WORK IN SELFRIDGES in London and they asked me to do some modelling while I was there. I also worked for a charity called the Oasis Trust, which works with homeless people here and in such places as India and Brazil. I'd love to visit India – I've never been and I'd love to see it.

6

WE'VE ALWAYS HAD CATS IN MY FAMILY. This is Mittens, who is about five years old now. Mittens is the fourth cat we've had and now we're up to number six!

7

8

I'VE ALWAYS LOVED SPORT and here I am finishing my first London Marathon last year. I ran it in three and a half hours. I also love keeping fit and playing football. Another thing I'd love to do on Blue Peter is spend a day training with my favourite football team, Norwich City Football Club.

49

Take a look at
Katy's Big Day

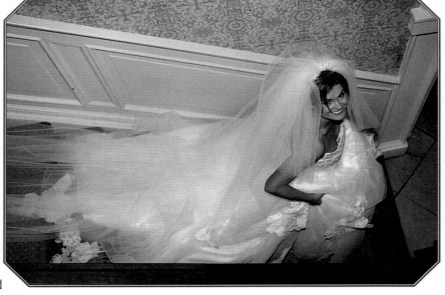

On a romantic weekend in Paris, Katy was asked, "Will you marry me?". "Yes!" she told her boyfriend of twelve years, Andrew Frampton. Katy could hardly wait to show off her engagement ring and let everyone know her news. She even shared it with Blue Peter viewers as soon as she could and in her excitement sang "I'm getting married in the morning", giving lots of people the wrong idea!

It wasn't long before Katy's big day arrived for real. On Saturday 13 March at 11 o'clock, Katy and her dad sat side by side in a horse-drawn carriage as it pulled up outside the pretty church of St Mary's in Hadleigh, Suffolk.

Katy wore the most gorgeous white wedding gown, with a bodice covered in silk ivy leaves, and a three-metre train held in place by a diamond-encrusted tiara. Her bouquet was of arum lilies and ferns. Miss Katy Hill walked down the aisle with her dad and after the marriage ceremony walked out of the church as Mrs Andrew Frampton.

The wedding ceremony was witnessed by the Frampton and Hill families as well as close friends – not forgetting Stuart, Konnie, Simon and ex-Blue Peter presenter, Diane-Louise Jordan.

Katy and Andrew flew off for a romantic honeymoon in Bali. Katy returned to Blue Peter two weeks later, looking tanned and radiantly happy. She also came armed with a tier of her wedding cake, for all the gang in the BP office. We all tucked in, wishing Katy and Andrew every happiness in the future.

Recycled Wedding Dress

This was what Katy wore on her first programme as Mrs Frampton – a wonderful wedding dress that was just a bit different from hers. The dress was made from plastic carrier bags and the outfit came complete with train, headdress, underskirt and a bouquet. The unusual wedding gown was the work of Bradford-based designer Christine Hughes, who had scrunched, gathered and sewn 250 bags together to create it.

COUNTDOWN TO THE

There are certainly going to be some huge celebrations going on at the end of this year to mark the start of the new millennium. But as well as joining in with the festivities, the Blue Peter team has also got some hard work ahead of them digging up the time capsules that are buried somewhere in the Blue Peter garden.

The first box full of souvenirs of the programme was buried on 7 June 1971 by presenters Valerie Singleton, John Noakes and Peter Purves. At that time, the millennium seemed ages away – 29 years!

The lead-lined box had to be moved on 30 March 1984 before the land at the front of Television Centre was dug up and developed. So the new Blue Peter presenters, Simon Groom, Peter Duncan and Janet Ellis, buried it along with a second time capsule in a secret location somewhere in the Blue Peter garden.

We should be able to find them quite easily thanks to the map in the vaults of the BBC's bank which shows the exact location the boxes for the Year 2000 are buried. And if you don't know what's inside our capsules, you'll just have to make sure you tune in and watch the programme!

Top: Way back in 1971 presenters John and Peter, with a little help from Petra, the Blue Peter dog, buried a time capsule at the front of Television Centre to be dug up in the year 2000.
Above: Peter and Valerie seal up the special lead-lined box which was made by the BBC's Props Department.
Right: A year later the presenters measure the silver birch tree which was planted to mark the spot.

MILLENNIUM!

More recently, on 11 June 1998, we buried the Blue Peter Millennium Time Capsule in the floor beneath the Millennium Dome in Greenwich. The capsule contains various Blue Peter items such as a set of badges and a booklet about the history of the programme. We also launched a competition asking viewers to choose something that would inform the next generation of what was important to them in the late twentieth century. Two thousand of the best entries, as well as the twelve objects suggested by the top winners, were also placed in the capsule. All the entries were put on to computer so that you can visit the Dome when it opens in December 1999 and look at them while the real thing is lying deep in the earth below.

Above: Bad news in 1984 – the box has to be moved because a car park is being built at Television Centre: Peter, Simon and Janet get stuck in moving the tree and the box for the year 2000 to a new, secret location in the Blue Peter garden.
Left: Not to miss a trick – they buried a second time capsule.
Top: 1998 and another quite spectacular time capsule is lowered into the ground.

STUART'S MAGIC

I've had so many great adventures on Blue Peter that it's been quite hard to choose my magic moments but here goes!

One of the best things about being a Blue Peter presenter is you never know what you're going to be asked to do next. I've ridden on top of the human pyramid with the Flying Gunners motorcycle display team, whizzed down the Cresta Run and even helped to mend the King Kong ride at Universal studios in California. One of my most thrilling experiences was when Dave Roberts took me speed gliding – it's a fast and furious sport and definitely not one for the nervous! At one point Dave let me have control of the glider. Steering it was a lot easier than I imagined – you pull the weight of your body to the left to go left and to the right to go right. Simple! It was an amazing feeling to go gliding through the air at such a speed and the views of the Welsh countryside were beautiful. It was one of those rare occasions on Blue Peter when I've been left speechless!

I've been lucky enough to travel the world, visiting many fantastic places. But the country that's most special for me is Brazil which I travelled to for the Blue Peter 1996 Appeal. We were raising money to help people suffering from 'the world's oldest disease', leprosy – people like 14-year-old Adriana who told me "My friends treat me badly, they say awful things to me.

Stuart at Biggin Hill Air Show before taking part in a display with the RAF Falcons. He was the first civilian ever to do so.

This left me speechless – speed gliding in Wales with Dave Roberts.

After speeding through the air, I was glad to make a safe landing.

They make me feel like an outcast." Thanks to the hard work of Blue Peter viewers we managed to raise enough money to provide mobile treatment units with 28 jeeps, 32 motorbikes and 118 bicycles as well as a new leprosy clinic in Ceara, Brazil and a new laboratory and operating treatment units in Hyderbad, India. I realised how special Blue Peter appeals are and how they really can make a difference.

I love animals and have had many fascinating encounters with all sorts of creatures during my time on the programme. One of my most thrilling moments was when I helped relocate Tembo, a five-ton elephant, in Kenya with the Born Free Foundation. Having been transported in a box for 24 hours, Tembo was very angry when he came out and charged our landrover. Fortunately, he moved off into the bush when our driver turned on the car engine! And I'll never forget the time I came face to face with one of the world's most famous but threatened creatures, the Mountain Gorillas of Uganda. After tracking through the rainforest for hours, my heart started to beat really fast when I caught sight of some.

Ship ahoy – me beside HMS Victory in Portsmouth.

It was a real privilege they allowed us to sit so close to them and watch them eat and play. I was incredibly nervous when the huge silver-back gorilla approached us – he could have been on top of us in a couple of seconds. Fortunately he lost interest and went off for a sleep! I could have stayed and watched them for hours and hours and was really sad when I was told it was time to go – I felt I'd only been there for 5 minutes. It was certainly the most incredible experience I've had on Blue Peter.

My proudest moment on Blue Peter has to be the time I jumped into the history books as the first civilian to take part in a full public display with the RAF Falcons at the Biggin Hill Air Show. Fortunately the free-fall and linking up with the members of the Falcons in the stack all went well. And once we'd landed, we then had to quickly take off our parachutes and stand in line as an RAF Hercules flew past in salute over our heads. It still makes my spine tingle!

I had to keep my balance on top of the Flying Gunners' moving pyramid.

Stuart in accelerated free-fall with instructors from RAF Weston-on-the-Green.

This was the moment Tembo the elephant was released from his box.

Me and Will in Kenya with elephant truck E-17.

CHOCOLATE TRUFFLES

If you're planning a celebration – a birthday, Christmas or even passing an exam – there's nothing better than something rich, smooth and deliciously chocolatey to share with friends. These might look like extravagant hand-made chocs, but looks can be deceptive. Just follow this recipe and you'll see that chocolates don't have to cost the earth.

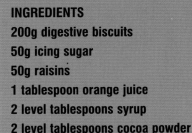

INGREDIENTS
200g digestive biscuits
50g icing sugar
50g raisins
1 tablespoon orange juice
2 level tablespoons syrup
2 level tablespoons cocoa powder
100g butter

SUGGESTED DECORATION
chocolate strands (vermicelli),
desiccated coconut,
icing sugar mixed with a little water,
pieces of glacé cherries or angelica

METHOD
- Crush the biscuits in a bowl. Add the icing sugar, raisins and orange juice and mix together.
- Melt the butter, syrup and cocoa powder in a small saucepan over a gentle heat. Stir until melted. Remove from the heat and add to the other ingredients in the bowl. Mix well.
- Form the mixture into small ball shapes.
- Put the truffles into small cake cases.
- Put these on a baking sheet and place in the fridge for about 2 hours.
- If you're making truffles for Christmas you could decorate them as mini-puddings by making up some white icing and spreading it on top. The icing should be thick, not runny. Decorate with small pieces of glacé cherries and angelica to look like holly leaves and berries.
- Alternatively, roll some truffles in a bowl of chocolate strands or in a bowl of coconut before chilling in the fridge.
- The truffles make delicious presents and look good gift-wrapped in cellophane, tied up with ribbon. You could even make a chocolate box and display the truffles on cut-up strands of tissue paper.

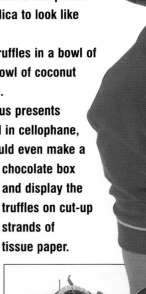

Warning – once you start eating these you may not be able to stop!

56

MATT BAKER

25 June 1999 and the 28th Blue Peter presenter was welcomed to the team and introduced to Blue Peter viewers.

Born	**Friday 23 December 1977, in Easington Village**
Height	**1.78m**
Home town	**Durham**
Star sign	**Capricorn**

FAVOURITES...

Colour	**Blue**
Best food	**Sunday dinner**
Worst food	**Macaroni cheese**
Sports	**Most sports, especially gymnastics, football, snooker and tennis**
Band	**The Corrs**
Album	**James Bond themes**
TV Shows	**Ground Force and the Dukes of Hazzard**
Star	**Steve Martin/Leslie Nielsen**
Best Movie	**Ferris Bueller's Day Off**
Clothes	**Combats, big boots and Levi checked shirt**
Best ways to spend Saturdays	**At home on the farm with my family and dogs**

BEGINNINGS...

Family	**1 sister, 2 stepsisters**
Schools	**Easington Village Church of England Junior and Infants School; Belmont Comprehensive; Durham Sixth-Form Centre; Queen Margaret's University College, Edinburgh**
Favourite subjects	**Art and PE**
Hated subjects	**French and Chemistry**
Qualifications	**8 GCSEs, 3 'A' levels, Diploma in Acting, Community Sports Leader Award, First-Aid Certificate**
Earliest ambition	**To compete in the Olympics with the Great Britain gymnastic team**
First acting experience	**Pugsley in the junior school production of The Addams Family**
Hobbies when younger	**Gymnastics (British Squad), sheepdog training, sports acrobatics, drawing and climbing trees!**
Pets when younger	**St Bernard (Cromwell), 2 Giant Schnauzers (Shogun and Flossey), 3 sheepdogs (Lale, Meg and Fern), cats Phoenix, Shar, Tom and Pebbles, as well as hamsters, rabbits, guinea pigs and fish**
First job	**Early morning milk round**

TOMORROW...

Most wants to do on BP	**Apart from lighting the Blue Peter Christmas advent candle, I'd like to learn to be a stuntman**
Country most wants to visit	**Africa – the jungle**
People most respect	**My dad**
Bad habits	**Eating biscuits very loudly and being very untidy**
Ambition	**It was to be a Blue Peter presenter, but now it's just to be happy, successful and have no regrets**

→How to win your

Be the envy of your friends! Be the envy of your parents who always wanted one. Get in free at hundreds of places all over Britain. In other words, win a Blue Peter badge! There are five different badges – Gold, Silver, Blue, Green and Competition.

What makes Blue Peter badges extra-special is that they have to be won.
Way back in 1962 when Biddy Baxter and Edward Barnes produced the programme, they invented the Blue Peter badge. The idea was that viewers should wear their badges with pride. They had to be *won* and were never given away. Many important people have been upset and offended over the years because they were not given badges for themselves or for their children. The simple rule still applies today, which is why winning a Blue Peter badge is still special.

Green badges started in 1988.
We award them for letters, pictures or poems about wildlife and the environment. We love to hear what you are doing to improve your surroundings or your views on environmental problems at home and abroad.

Competition badges look different to the other shield-shaped badges.
They're awarded to winners and runners-up in our competitions. We hold lots of competitions throughout the year – some are harder than others – but if you don't enter, you don't stand a chance of winning a badge!

Winning a Blue Peter badge isn't difficult, though.
Just by writing 'Dear Blue Peter...' you could win the most famous badge of all, a Blue one. The presenters usually wear Blue badges and we award them to children under 16 who send us an interesting letter, an idea for the programme, a recipe, a picture, a poem or a story. If you ever take part in the programme, this is the badge you'll win.

Gold badges are our highest award.
Even if you have won a Blue, Silver, Green and Competition badge, you are not automatically entitled to win a Gold one next. Gold badges are rare and only a handful are awarded each year. You will only win one if you do something extraordinary like saving someone's life (witnesses needed)!

Blue badge winners who also want to win a Silver have to do something different.
If you won your Blue badge for sending us a photograph of something you made, you could then send us a mouth-watering recipe, to win a Silver badge.

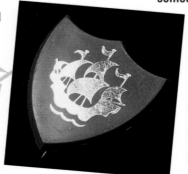

The only thing we do not award badges for is helping with our Appeals.
We don't think anyone should expect a reward for helping others. However, there are so many ways to win a Blue Peter badge that we're sure you'll succeed if you try! Good luck!

Blue Peter badge

Exploris – an exploration of the Irish Sea in Portaferry in Northern Ireland. Definitely worth a top stop-off to find out more.

You can visit the SS Great Britain built by Isambard Brunel. It was the first iron built steamship driven by a screw propeller and it is now being restored where she was built – in Bristol's Great Western Dockyard.

There are fabulous views from the top of the Scottish Lighthouse Museum in Fraserburgh in Aberdeenshire.

➔ BADGE SQUAD –
some places you can visit FREE!

Blue Peter badges are not giveaways. Oh no! You have to win one and *that's* what makes the badge and the wearer special. There isn't a Blue Peter Club in the true sense of the word, but people who've been awarded badges often feel part of a club. We're not sure how many badge winners are out there but, after almost forty years of awarding them, it's probably close to one million.

Syon Park is in Brentford in Middlesex, and a great place for a picnic. Apart from the fabulous house, there is plenty to see – an aquatic experience and a butterfly sanctuary.

If you haven't already pinned on a Blue Peter badge, then look at the opposite page, get cracking and come up with a way to win yours. There's another great advantage to being a badge winner – there are loads of places all over the British Isles and even in Europe where you can get in free. So wherever you live or wherever you visit you'll probably find somewhere wonderful to go, where Blue Peter badge winners get free admission. New badge winners receive a leaflet with all the places listed and here are just a few.

If there's anyone over sixteen reading this, sorry, but the free entry offer doesn't apply to you any more!

Get in free to Sea-Life Centres which are all over the British Isles – there are also some in Europe.

You can talk to the chimps at Monkey World at Wareham in Dorset.

BEHIND THE SCENES

Most Blue Peter programmes start with an empty studio – a bit like an aircraft hangar. Find out how the studio's transformed when we get the show on the air.

MONDAY

Planning a Friday show starts first thing on Monday morning. The team meet in the Blue Peter office, and after a quick chat about the last programme they quickly start thinking about the next one. What ideas do we have? What's the film story? Is there a pop band in the show? The producer then puts all the ingredients down in a running order, deciding how much time each item will take and in which order they should appear. Then it's back to the phones and the computers to start researching, writing and booking everything and everybody!

TUESDAY

Tuesday – and the director starts working on a studio plan. No two Blue Peter programmes are ever the same, and it's up to the director to decide on how the Blue Peter set is arranged, depending on who or what's coming into the studio. A scale model helps give the director and designer a good idea of how everything will look.

WEDNESDAY

Wednesday – and it's a technical planning meeting. The Friday team meet the technical people who'll be organising the lighting, sound and cameras in the studio. The director explains what's going to happen and together they work out what kind of cameras are needed, what colours to light the set with and how many microphones are needed – depending on how many guests we have.

Top left: The director works out where to put the set, while the designer, Ross (above), sketches ideas for what the Batman area will look like.
Middle: In the lighting gallery, final touches are put to the way the set will be lit and whether the colours look good.
Right: Each camera has cards with a list of the different shots they will be asked to do.

Top left: Thursday night and the camera scripts are printed, ready for distribution by the PA.
Above: Friday morning and the final touches are made to Stuart's costume.
Top right: The script is put on to computer and the portaprompt operator can make changes during the day so that the team can read it on small screens hung underneath the camera lens.
Below: Up in the production gallery the vision mixer, director, PA and producer keep an eye on camera rehearsals and talk to the presenters through tiny earpieces.

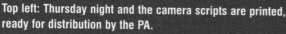

THURSDAY

Thursday – and it's time to start transforming the empty studio. First things first: paint the floor. As it's Friday, the floor is pale blue. There are no fancy machines or high technology involved in this job, just good old-fashioned elbow grease and a very big paint roller. When the paint is dry, the set is brought into the studio and placed exactly where the director has planned. And Friday just wouldn't be Friday without the star cloth that stretches around the set! This is like lots of giant curtains, covered in tiny pea lights which can flash on and off.

FRIDAY

The Big Day, and eight hours to rehearse so that everyone – cameramen, lighting and sound technicians, presenters – know exactly what's going to happen and when. During the studio lunch break, final touches are made to the set and lighting. Thirty minutes before going on air, and Mabel, Lucy, Kari and Oke arrive in the studio. Two minutes to go and the red lights start flashing outside the studio. The entire studio crew are in position, waiting to hear the Production Assistant count '... five, four, three, two, one, zero'. Blue Peter is live on air.

And that's all there is to it! So next time you watch, you'll know exactly what's been going on behind the Blue Peter scenes!

WIN A DAY OUT at the BLUE PETER STUDIO!

The answer to our competition question can be found in this book:

On what date was the first ever Blue Peter time capsule buried?

The winner, with friend and family (maximum 4 persons), will be able to spend a day with members of the Blue Peter team in the studio. The winner's transport costs to the studio will be provided.

- Competition entries must be received by 28 January 2000.
- Venue and visit date will be agreed with the winner.
- The winner will be notified by post no later than 1 March 2000.
- Send your answer, along with your name, age and address to:

Blue Peter Millennium Competition, Egmont World Limited, Deanway Technology Centre, Wilmslow Road, Handforth, Cheshire SK9 3FB.

- *REMEMBER! COMPETITION CLOSING DATE IS 28 JANUARY 2000.*

RULES
1 Entrants must be under 16 years of age.
2 One winner will be chosen at random and notified by post.
3 The judges' decision will be final. No correspondence can be entered into.
4 A list of winners will be made available on request from Egmont World Limited, Deanway Technology Centre, Wilmslow Road, Handforth, Cheshire SK9 3FB after 28 January 2000. Please enclose a s.a.e.
5 Employees (and their relatives) of Egmont World Limited and their associated companies are not eligible to enter.
6 Entries are limited to one per person.
7 Competition is open to residents of the UK, Ireland and the Channel Islands.
8 The publishers reserve the right to vary the prize, subject to availability.